LINEAGE

Of

A

COUNTRY

BOY

Lineage of a Country Boy
Copyright © 2014 Nolan Turner (Blacklife)

All rights reserved. Except for use in any review, the reproduction or utilization of this work in whole or in part in any form by any electronic, mechanical or other means, now known or hereafter invented, including xerography, photocopying and recording, or in any information storage or retrieval system, is forbidden without the written permission of the author, Nolan Turner, BlackLife. He can be reached at kristionalexande@yahoo.com.

All pictures are printed with permission and courtesy of the Lawrence and Turner family.

"The Days" is printed with permission and courtesy of MacKenzie Martin-Turner.

"I AM" is printed with permission and courtesy of Kristion Martin-Turner.

ISBN: 10:0692315330
ISBN-13:9780692315330

Authored by Nolan Turner (BlackLife)
Edited by Chay Sanders
Cover by KRose Designs

Lineage – a lineal descent from an ancestor or ancestry

Country – the land of a person's birth, residence or citizenship

Introduction to the
Lineage of a Country Boy

I grew up excited about summers going south to spend with my grandparents. So many life lessons were learned with any situation experienced good and bad times I am proud to say my good unquestionably outweighs anything that would be considered bad.

So many times and festive memories created through loving family and fond moments. Get togethers, reunions, and just great family dinners were enjoyed by family and friends. With prayer always being the start of any meal we partaken. To that family up bringing I remained grateful because I learned so much from the small church setting to the school sitting on a campus type environment. By no means have I forgotten my city influences but I experienced a night and day atmosphere between the two.

Unfortunately, we often forget the life lessons of our elders, the things that molded us into the people we have become or should have been. These lessons I experienced growing up from my Big Momma (Great-Grand), Momma (Grandma) and my Ma (Mother). I definitely can't forget Busta (Granddaddy) who surrounded me with a VILLAGE of people whose influences and little town southern ways helped mold a hard headed but well rounded boy from the city. A city that taught me to hustle and concrete lessons from my dad and friends.

Living in the country, this boy learned and experienced things some would only daydream about. From the fresh morning air, the sound of farm animals, crickets at dusk to complete southern hospitality and respect. I'm daydreaming now just reminiscing about good times. The city's concrete streets, sounds of violence, seeing drug sales, prostitution, the vacant lots where I once played to the cardboard boxes I used to break dance on. A lot of love was displayed from the North to the South of I-75 along with heartache but I survived to pass my life experiences and memories to my children in hopes of them creating their own dreams.

DEDICATION

First I would like to thank the Lord for all He continues to do for me. He wakes me up every morning and keeps me protected with the blood of His mighty son Jesus Christ. He has given me the talent and drive to complete not one book project but three. I give all praise and honor to my Lord. I would like to thank:

My Gramps Roosevelt Lawrence (RIP) for assisting in my development as a man;

My Grandmother Nettie Lee Lawrence (RIP) for nurturing and caring for me in my major times of need;

Ruby Jewel (Lawrence) Turner (RIP) for playing all the roles a mother could play. Although she didn't know all the roles she made a valiant effort;

Nathan J. Turner since in every situation something is learned therefore I use these as learning experiences.

I also like to thank all my aunties, uncles and elders, all of whom have crossed my path.

To everyone, I say "THANK YOU"! I love you all from the depth of my soul....

**Pen to paper
thoughts unloaded
everybody has a story
to be told**

**Close your eyes and allow
yourself to go down memory lane**

TABLE OF CONTENTS

Introduction to a Lineage of a Country Boy	4
Dedication	6
I am He	12
Four Hundred	14
Influenced	16
Never Forget	17
Church	18
In the Window	19
Oatmeal	20
Your Eyes Were Closed	21
Memories of Yesterday	22
Past	23
Ghetto	25
Whatever Happened	27
Generation Blackface	28
February	29
Changed	31
Tree	32

TABLE OF CONTENTS

If	33
One Wish	34
Rewind (Let Go and Live)	35
Remembering Home	37
The Old Wise Man	39
Listen to Me	40
A Stranger's Watching	41
Don't Forget	43
I Am a Man	44
Announcement	45
Blackman	46
Life Time Bid	47
Stages	48
Aging	49
Honor Thy Woman	50
Raised	52
Where I'm Going	54
Think	55

TABLE OF CONTENTS

No Mo'	56
My Deepest Fear	57
Funeral Reunion	58
Two Minutes	59
Home	60
Historical Oak	61
Perfect Dinner	62
I Am	65
The Days	66
Family Record	67

Nolan Turner

I AM HE

Made in His form
Pain running through my veins of those whose suffering
As I beg for the forgiveness of the forgotten
While praying for my sins and those surrounding me
Hopeful for the new day to bring purity
Sadden by the ones who don't believe in me
Enriched by my Father's belief in me
Tearful of the souls that came before me
Confused of why they lay in death in front of me
Understanding that my purpose has not yet been achieved
Not just in the physical form was I model
My heart beats of the rhythm that soothes an infant's cry
Relieves any child's pain from scrapes and bruises
Takes away the hurt of the battered woman
Redeeming the man's faith in family
Reinsuring the elderly that we as young legacies will not fail
Possessing the will to show the way to the blind
Creating faith to the non believers
Convincing the cripple that the journey can still be conquered
Helping the wrong doers to right their wrongs
Provide shelter to the homeless
Bring back the village to protect our children
Let them know we are there
As their shield and guide
Not predators and lovers
Bring the communities back together
Through strength and determination
Casting into the will of others to do great things
Preparing all around me to withstand the storm
Replacing children having baby
With children having diplomas
Remedying drug addiction

I AM HE

POWER is what I bring to you
Turn your back no more
Nor shall I to the Evil that stands before us
And the way of our grace and belief
Bring back the good that is hidden in the darkness
Removing the evil that has taken our light
Parents take your place as providers
Allowing children to have their youthful virginity
Children take your place on the timeline of life
Move slowly for that time can be remembered but not altered
People righteously create that prepared historical
monument for our future
Not teddy bears and R.I.P. signs in the communities
Bring prayer back to the English language
Instead of ignorance of Ebonics acceptance
Welfare assistance
Does not mean public dependence
Use what you've been blessed with
Do not use your blessing to be slaves of a remodeled plantation
Quit being bought with pennies and see your riches
Instead of prisons and case numbers
Claim and own your name given from your parents through God
Teach and prepare your children
So slave shackles won't have them lockdown
Due to illiteracy and lack of self respect
Recognize the value of what you create
Don't abuse or ignore the heir to your thrown
We need to get back to reading the word
Instead of disgracing the word
We are He in His word
With this we will successfully create a complete paradise
In our place along side of our Father and ancestors
In the Kingdom above!

Nolan Turner

FOUR HUNDRED

Four hundred years
Four hundred years
Four hundred years and we are still complaining that we're being wrong
Plymouth Rock landed on us, but four hundred years
Later we're smoking that rock
Selling that rock to one another in these streets
We treat the rock like Prudential all of us want a piece
Using "by any means necessary" as our slogan to achieve this stupidity

Four hundred years
Four hundred years
Four hundred years we are still fighting but not for rights
But for the entertainment of a betting society that believes with a bell
We will fight just like the way you train animals to respond
"Sit boy sit" ring the bell and say "good boy"
"Scrub harder nappy root girl" ring the bell and say "good girl"
Say the word they'll kill one another

Four hundred years
Four hundred years
Four hundred years retirement plans are being offered
"What you got on it", nothing but you got five on a "nickel" bag
You put in on that gin and juice
You claim they killing us but you put in on that abortion
To help rid our race, our purpose and our people

If extinction is what they want, we are working hard to give it to them
Took us out the field and into the streets of the ghetto
Where we work just as hard as if we were picking cotton
We are no longer singing Negro spirituals
Now we are rapping ignorant in your windows

Four hundred years
Four hundred years
Instead of "let my people go" and "wading in the water"

FOUR HUNDRED

It's "that's my boy, he's cool" while handling that 10 year bid
or pouring out a lil liquor

Let's STOP
Stop giving our minds away for a piece of white candy
Stop giving our freedom away for 26 inches of chrome
Stop giving our life away for a quick way to live

Four hundred years
Four hundred years
Four hundred years ago we could smile as the years
Came to pass from what was accomplished
What will the generations to come have to say if they still existed?

INFLUENCED

I sat at the dining room table at 4:30 in the morning
Drinking coffee at the tender age of six years young

Planning out long hours of the morning
Trying to complete it all before out comes
 the hot rays of the morning sun

I sat at the junk house as you taught me how to oil tools
Listening to the crow of the rooster waking up the late bird
Coon dogs sitting by our sides as the morning dew dried away
Smiling as I hung on to your every word
I sat on the side of the house by your side
Shelling peas, chewing on tobacco and skeeting it
through the gap in my teeth

Country air could only smell better if I were the wind itself
Wearing our straw hats cause from the sun we used to hide
I walked in your footsteps one hole, one seed at a time in the garden
It seems as if the path would never end
Sipping on lemonade out of mason jars as sweat dripped off our brows

Having the opportunity to know you as my Gramps, Pops and friend
And then in front of you I sat; a task that came easier to me
than I expected
Trying to hold back tears as death continues to feel new to me
Standing tall when asked to help guide your body to its final rest

Gramps, even gone, you've prepped me for any situation to be my best!

NEVER FORGET

As the summer grows to a close and the days become longer
anticipation of the night air lingers in my mind

Anxious like a school boy awaiting the last bell of the year to ring
hoping everything I imagine would come true this summer

The chairs at the table filled with love ones, laughing
and joking with memories of yesterday

Listening to old school tales or hearing jokes
that was only funny way back when

Arguing over whose music was better as someone always had
to get up and do their favorite dance step

Even when the party ended for the children,
the music would continue to play in our dreams

Realizing as the years went on the advice past on
serves more purpose than you would ever know

Understanding more now why enjoying being a child
was treasured memories and not to be taken for granted

Or being told to be the best you can
and you will see the rewards come back two-folds

Memories that are not just memories but more like a mental scrapbook
to be passed on through generations

So we not only will be able to teach our children
but also never forget from where the lessons came from

Nolan Turner

CHURCH

Sunday early in the morning greeted by church hymns
Standing in the shower as I stretched out all my limbs

Button up, dress slacks and tight shoes I barely wore
Rushing to finish my oatmeal so I could hurry out the door

Chubby lil' legs walking double time to my siblings every one step
Sometimes running to keep up so I wouldn't get left

Just a lil' ole church sitting on a dusty gravel road
Hearing about the stories in the Bible and the way they were told

Pennies jingling around the room as the collection plate was passed
Yes those were the days when you wish service would last

Days when the congregation would gather for Baptism at the river
And as a child watching the spirit takeover making me shake and shiver

Ole southern back road lil' building is where religion began
Southern hospitality where every day was family and friends

Lineage of A Country Boy

IN THE WINDOW

Often there are times when we run into parents who neglects their responsibility as parents. Children find themselves playing make believe with themselves and creating imaginary friends and even than they never see the means to the end.....

I'm in the window
Smiling cause you called and said you'll be here
I even invited my friends over to meet you
Every day I talk about you but some don't even think you exist
So I had to shut them up, it was only a three day suspension
Don't worry I made up the work, my smarts I got from you

Still in the window
No, no you're not late I'm just anxious for you to arrive
Here awaiting your gift to me
not that I need it but you said I would like it
wondering if it's that toy from my birthday or Christmas
It don't matter it's a gift from you that's all I need

Even though I'm being told to get out the window
I'm still in the window
My heart is racing now any moment you should be here
I see cars coming but maybe you're in a truck
or maybe you're real cool and you're riding a motorcycle or a big hog
Wow, my friends will really dig that

It's getting late, I haven't left the window
My faith in you is stronger than you know
Although my friends had to go home
The night has grown over the sky
Its past my bedtime, I called you with no answer
"Baby don't cry"
"But Daddy, Momma promised"

OATMEAL

To this day I couldn't figure out why oatmeal tasted so good
Why in the morning the anticipation consumed me and I couldn't wait to get to the table

It wasn't the raisins that flavored the oats while they were cooking
nor the brown sugar that bubbled and simmered around the top of the pot

I don't even think the butter melting around the sides was the answer
or the pet milk that poured down like a fountain to cool it down
Nor my special bowl or spoon that I ate every last drop with

Thirty-four years later, I finally realized it was 'you' that worked midnights but still had breakfast on the table

That sang church hymns while preparing morning meals

Praying over each meal with the family before eating

Making sure no one left the table until they were full
Hugs and kisses before off to school we went running

Just to do it all over again the next day after day
Oatmeal taste so good because you prepared it with LOVE!

YOUR EYES WERE CLOSED

So many thoughts went through my mind as I held back the tears

Standing tall, chest out as I were taught when facing my fears

Laughing to myself, as I remembered fun times

I'm sure people thought I was crazy

The way I used to tease the oldest two cause I was your baby

I manned up, took care of business the way you always taught me to

Never knowing the business I would handle would one day be for you

With a lump in my throat, my head held high

Your baby boy took care of your needs

And on rainy days, when the sun shines like your smile,

I smile knowing you are pleased and at rest

With memories of no pain and suffering eased my heart

Nevertheless, missing you and all you did

When I thought you were over mothering

So I carry you in my heart

As new lessons approaches and memories unfolds

I am blessed to have had you before your eyes were closed

Nolan Turner

MEMORIES OF YESTERDAY

If I could dream one dream
I would be back on my green machine
Hitting switches on that old country back road
Yeah that's right, that road where I used to play
It feels good to have memories of that yesterday

Red light, green light, being chased through those old fields
Chillin' in the back of that heavy Chevy pickup truck
Gravel crackling under the tires, while in the back I lay
It feels good to have memories of that yesterday

Straw hat matching that one worn by my Elder
Picking dinner out of the garden as the dew dissolves on the ground
Walking bare feet unknowingly as my ancestors did
It feels good to have memories of that yesterday

Roosters interrupting your dreams with their morning serenades
The scent of fresh brewed coffee sailing through the air
Time to get up a new day is starting as the wise man used to say
It feels good to have memories of that yesterday

As the school bus arrived at the corner for pick ups
Excited to see that teacher, who with a smile, could get you to work
Running home from the bus stop to discuss your day
It feels good to have memories of that yesterday

And as age catches us, cause it always does
Children grow up and move out and on with their own lives
Family reminiscing about all the good ole days
I'll smile knowing I have memories of yesterday

Lineage of A Country Boy

PAST

I'm so excited, can't wait to see this lady
This day couldn't come any sooner; she got pictures of my baby

Barber came so you know I had to get a trim
And my people looked out so I'm wearing fresh new Timbs

Ahh man here she come, can she see my face light up
How come she's not smiling something's wrong or messed up?

She's walking real slowly, with no eye contact
I'm starting to feel uneasy; I'm normally chilled and laid back

As she gets up on me I know something must be wrong
The mood was so dreary; I could hear old Negro slave songs

The room became dark I could see mouths moving
but there was pure silence
I was looking down, seeing preparation of the choir list

Momma breaking down from the kiss on the forehead
not knowing any better I'd say someone was dead

Pure silence, slave songs, choir list; hell to the naw
This morning I was brushing my teeth standing proud and tall

Pain in my back, that wasn't there before
feel like I've been hit, I can feel it for sure

Wait a moment let me re-cap, naw I don't see nothing outta place
Let me go to the mirror and rinse my face

But the reflection I was expecting to see is no longer there
I'm not understanding; this situation is crazy
Mama what's up with this color something I would never wear

Nolan Turner

PAST

Hold up I gotta be tripping ain't nothing right about this scene
I'm right here Mama why she acting like I can't be seen

Cries drown out from the sounds of horses headed my way
As I begin to focus up, I realized I was experiencing my judgment day

From a faint recap I could hear a voice say this breathe is your last
Now I too am a memory of the past...
.

GHETTO

Take my hand, close your eyes
I promise I won't fail you again
but I know of a place
surrounded by a concrete jungle
it's a pure paradise
in the hell of the ghetto

Watch your step, the broken glass and the needles
and the cats in the walkways
Follow me
I promise I won't do you wrong anymore
with the respect for my mother
the same for you I'll show

So follow me to this paradise
where the two mystical flowers of forever dwell
through riots, poverty and drugs
they maintain, remain and will flourish
watching all the tragic things that occurs
murder, rape and sadness

Come with me do not be afraid
I need you to believe in me
as I will you
with no one between the two
Allow me to prove myself worth
honoring, supporting and loving you completely
let's be like my mystical flowers
loving deeply

GHETTO

Ghetto paradise where all our Grandfathers –
Honored
Loved
Respected
Cared
Supported
Pampered
and put before all
The LORD
and
their women

Ghetto paradise where all our Grandmothers –
Loved
Honored
Respected
Cared
Supported
Cleaned
Cooked
and put before all the LORD
and
their men

WHATEVER HAPPENED

Whatever happened to the good ole days?
    Not the hip hop phase
    or the used jeans craze

Whatever happened to the good ole days?
    Not the Gumby cuts
    or the "we" was doing the "butt"

Whatever happened to the good ole days?
    Not he kick ball in the street
    or the break dancing to the beat

Whatever happened to the good ole days?
    Not the get off my bozaks
    or this beat is wack

Whatever happened to the good ole days?
    Not the dance the wop
    or DJ Magic Mike "Drop"

Whatever happened to the good ole days?
    Not the swim mobile
    or Guy's "Let's Chill"

Whatever happened to the good ole days of FAMILY?

Nolan Turner

GENERATION BLACKFACE

Here I thought the days of Sambos and Blackface was long gone and shit
It's more prevalent now, then the days of that theatrical half ass wit
Still fucked up jokes and poor acting about the skin tone of my people
Bullshit insecurities and poor reactions from my race allowing this sequel

Shows put on to depict and present poor views
But no reality of the homeless on the evening news
Motherfuckas dressed in rags getting media attention
To busy focusing on minstrel shows acting out lynching

Black men walking round like hood Niggas or now hood figures so they say
We all gonna laugh at you is what the media shows us everyday
This society don't care about you but you can't see pass your eye lids
Instead of public auctions they're silent nevertheless still placing bids

Dickies saggin' walking around like there's shit in your pants
Blackface, automatically all you gotta do now is your dance
"Massa gone be proud of me y'all will see"
Black man getting locked up, continuing systematic slavery

Piling make-up all over your face spot light on you
Make-up covering each blow that turned you black and blue
Addicted to that stuff (blow, needle and those pills)
Choosing the destruction of your bodies instead of the right to live

Sambos, blackface, my people please step up your game
It's our time to be successful and stop being the puppet on the string
Generation blackfaces stop destroying your life by being the first to die
Quit allowing 'Massa' to feed you those lies

FEBRUARY

I grew up to the names of Dr. Martin Luther King Jr. who believed in nonviolence.

Malcolm X by any means necessary 'you'll hear my guns in the midst of silence'.

Madame C.J. Walker hot comb straightened those nappy Negro curls

How they blamed Emmitt Till's death on his own behavior because he should have never whistle at a white girl.

Harriett Tubman risked her life to free the slaves traveling through the underground.

Mrs. Rosa Parks was tired and refused to give up her seat to a white man after she sat down.

All these names are important as they stand out in history.

But society never touches on the strong Negro man who hung from the country tree.

Nor the ridicule and rape our beautiful sistas endured throughout the plantation.

Never speaking on the death by shock after a teenage African boy suffered castration.

Or all the unmarked graves cause African people meant NOTHING back in that time.

Everything that occurred back than wasn't allowed on the historical timeline.

FEBRUARY

Everybody that fought the battle wasn't remembered during the winning of the war.

And if you don't have Elders to gain knowledge from you're done

cause you won't find it in the book stores.

So don't get me wrong all these names are important and very necessary.

But we need to learn about more than just in the month of February!

CHANGED

We have replaced the word "**beauty**". A word that describes our ancestral mothers and daughters, with the word "bitch" degrading our women and allowing others to as we simply laugh as if it's okay.

Taking away the "**nor**" in "**Honor**" a meaning our women carried with pride; earned by them for their patience and the way they held down the family by taking up the slack when their men left home. But now we call them "hoes".

Physically our women have been raped, beaten and tortured. Still holding their heads up high and pushing on; showing their children that regardless of their tragedy what don't kill them definitely creates **strength**. No matter how we treat their body; our sluts they will never be.

Toying with the emotions of women and breaking their hearts. Displaying the behavior of a savage beast, imprinting on every woman soul we come across has caused our women to shelter their love. No longer having trust for the men they once called their **Kings**.

Not having a King has led them into the hands of fools and wayward men, leaving them confused for leadership so they seek out their own solution. As we become angered and accused them of questioning our manhood. They needed protection and we wasn't there. Answering our own question, we are not being **men**.

As men forgetting to respect our women has become a common trend. That has altered the beauty and essence of our women. Strength through our arrogant ways destroying the image of men in their eyes. The honor we didn't show completes the "**dysfunctional**" women with the protection we didn't provide.

Yet we call our women "**Queens**"!

Nolan Turner

TREE

I was watered and nurtured with all types of light
I was talked to, wiped and primed on a regular
I stood out blossoming year after year soaking it all in
Wouldn't allow myself to be weeded down at all
So I made sure my roots were strong enough to endure
Stormy days drowned me
droughts never made me thirsty
and because I am a branch from the tree
The pine tree that bared lots of seeds, some hung on and some dropped
the pine tree that cried of sap when sadden
from the wrong done to him
his production of greatness has neva been a question
Watching trees around him go through drama and suffering
not going without fault but strong enough to maintain through disparity
and as the pick of the bunch is pulled from the tree
You can tell what kind of tree it is by the quality that it bare

IF

If I were who I used to be
getting an education would have just been okay
Children out of wedlock would have continued to be my way
listening during a conversation with too much to say
Bad relationships would continue with drama being my servants pay
instead of divorce I would continue to allow abuse day by day
Risking being placed to rest as people view the site where I lay
while my children sleep at night wishing for their mother they pray
But I evolved no longer being weak in the soul where it controls my mind
Accepting who I was to prepare for the transformation of a new me
placing my faith in my God and not my mate
Speaking with a humble tongue and a forgiving heart
carrying the lesson of my daily teachings with me to grow and learn from
Praying over my problems and to my Lord I look for solutions
bringing my change, my purpose, my evolution

Nolan Turner

ONE WISH

If I had one wish, I would wish you never passed
so you could be here to see your son become a man at last

Witness the creation that were made with your characteristics

Smiling cause I listened well enough not to become another statistic

Being able to call you just to hear your opinions on Sundays

Instead of becoming emotional when I hear
Dianne Reeves song "Better Days"

Wishing I could return back home to see the glare of the porch light
Today I would welcome the noise; instead I hear the serenity
of the grave site

How things would have been different with your presence to guide me
It would help solve this confusion that I have been feeling lately

These emotions destroys minds while hurting the heart
like it's under attack
Now I really know about the meaning of days you can't get back

No matter how much I wish time would turn back reality stays the same
But I do know my memories of you will always remain

REWIND (LET GO AND LIVE)

Closing my eyes, the tape deck in my head has been placed on playback
remembering the days of family like a classic old skool track

The days where family was a simple Sunday morning phone call
cousins bragging about whose skills were better with b-ball

365 days we may not see each other face to face
but encouragement by phone or letters was a mental embrace

Counting the days to the summer to reunite with my southern life
all gathering in the same house no hatred, no sorrow and no spite

The buzz from the street lights calling you back home
listening to football games around the radio days all gone

Catching crawdads in the ditch on a rainy day was fun
hunting in the woods with homemade sling shots and BB guns

Hearing your name call from down the street with a commanding voice
full sprint with urgency cause you knew Poppa gave no options or choice

Respect with some fear of the unknown kept you in line
but as the saying goes those were the sign of the times

You know when family was family showing love was a necessity
now the focus through the years has become no fam, no us, just me

The nucleus has become little atoms of selfish behaviors
but allegedly we all believe in the same Lord and Savior

Nolan Turner

REWIND (LET GO AND LIVE)

When the aging of the mind stops no more assistance for help
souls so tainted your spirit roams but can't be felt

Stop the madness it only creates more pain and sorrow
living in the yesterday year instead of the now, the tomorrow

You only get ONE family ONE life time
and it can't always be spent on REWIND.....

REMEMBERING HOME

Collard greens and red beans is what

I like on my plate

Red or orange Kool-Aid is what I drink to quench my taste

Momma cooking up curry chicken and dumplings

and you know you gotta lace it over some rice

But brown rice is what I prefer to soothe my appetite

Grandma's tea cakes that was pressed down with that old bent fork

How we boys gathered around Gramps for the stories

 on the front porch

Watch out for that tin can with the tissue round the bottom

I tried a chew of that square block didn't know I couldn't swallow

"Me and you will never part" is how it felt when it was time to leave

"Fried sweated out chicken in a brown paper bag, Grandma please"

From 99 bottles of beer on the wall, to bingo on the red van

There was never a doubt in anyone's head about gatherings at the land

Pine Bluff, Arkansas whew it seems like everything is all gone

No more curry chicken, tea cakes or tin cans but their

memories still lives on

REMEMBERING HOME

I was blessed though to find my start,

new beginning and my mate

Just to have my son say to me, "Collard greens

and red beans is what I like on my plate"

THE OLD WISE MAN

"I've been there and done that"
Is what the old wise man was trying to say

I've heard your complaints and noted them all time and time again
Being your superior but trying not to forget to be a friend
Have led some in to battle and went into the trenches with a few
Treating all equal as any team player would attempt to do

Watching you test the waters but wondering
do you really think you're slick
Have you not realized that things you got away with
is because I created those tricks

Trying to show you that I once did the same things too
Explaining that the new tricks you've come up with aren't really new
I learned a lot, taught some to and was even willing to give
Now it's time for me to pass the torch and begin to live
Starting a new adventure never forgetting the past
But knowing it's time for someone else to take on this task
Hoping you've listened so your success can be greater than my own
Keeping your work family safe, no injuries to take home

Learn to enjoy all your situations don't let them get the best of you
And be sure of your decisions and always remain true
Respect yourself and those surrounding you everyday
So when the time comes you can be the old wise man
Is all I'm trying to say

Nolan Turner

LISTEN TO ME

I've seen hurt
I've been hurt

Know I will never cause you pain
I'm your protector; use me for what I am live life while it's offered
Don't turn your head pay full attention
It's important that you hear my words

My eyes have cried and seen enough tears to create flood rains
The souls of many aches through my veins causing me to yell out
Please listen to me I'm trying to tell you the truth
I've seen mothers and fathers destroyed from the death of their youth

Children destroyed because their parents don't spend time in the house
Cheating and cheating constantly done to their spouse
Death and dying, killing and murders in this concrete hell
Cats constantly going behind the walls content in jail

Babies never knowing their mommas because she's in the streets
Sons lacking understanding cause daddies are six feet deep
We use to look up family trees now we're smoking trees
Babies being born with infectious diseases

The world is pure chaos more than the eye can see
Because no one listened when Jesus said "Listen to me"

A STRANGER'S WATCHING

Streets were my introduction to manhood

or should I say man-mis-under-stood

You couldn't tell me 'ish probably wouldn't matter no way

wasting my time drinking with the boys blowing my day

Confused about life no real men to sit me down and explain

aging clock just a tickin' away while I find fault and place blame

"You should have been there, you could have taught me right"

but as the saying goes "another struggle another fight"

Another phone call how easily death creeps in the back door

Tears that burns your eyes from homies you'll see no more

Nightmares that plagues you at night thinkin' to yourself this

"ish is deep"

Waking up in sweats, cause you feeling closer to that 6 foot sleep

Insanity increases, every corner is a blurry road

"This is the world's fault I'm carrying the heavy load"

That's what I kept telling myself, which left me trapped

Awaken by a stranger, jumped up ready to bust a cap

Don't fear child you were only taking a rest

Heart beating fast as if it was about to jump out my chest

STRANGER'S WATCHING

Moving back nervously was a difference from being scared

He touched my shoulder and I begin to see hundreds

of years of pain he's bared

Blurred vision fading away as my focus begins to return

I could see the outcome of the lessons people didn't learn

Still at a loss for words cause he wouldn't let my shoulder go

even with my idle threats he provided some more

My shirt became wet where his hand were placed

blood was the substance running from his forehead to his face

The strength in his voice and power in hands brung me to my knees

as He stated,

"This will provide all your needs. I been watching you

and your answers were always there. The troubles you've

seen I gave you the will to bear. The tears and pain you've

faced was so your testimony would be fierce. Cause its

important that everyone stop to hear this."

Don't get me wrong as confused and nervous as I was

Speaking with volume, He said,

"Don't be scared because you're protected by my blood."

DON'T FORGET

Roses are red, yellow, peach, blue and a lot of other colors
Just like people you come across daily

Changing their appearance to become something they're not
So it will look better than what it is

When it's all said and done the rose is still a rose good or bad
And people are still people

When you get a rose, red or any other color you preserve them
But people you abuse, hurt and when their gone
You send roses or other colorful flowers

People are the only life form that doesn't respect life
The animal kingdom only takes what they need

People uses until it's all gone and don't share
Roses are red but people are God's creation

Nolan Turner

I AM A MAN

I am a man; you ask me how I know well I'll tell you...

My strong family ways and work ethics I received from Busta aka Roosevelt Lawrence who worked and took care of home. His hands got dirty and he fixed things when they were broken. He slaved for himself not others. He cried alone not to be seen.

I tend to the needs of my home....

Nettie Lee Lawrence from this I learned. Laundry was always done hung out on the line blowing in the wind. The aroma of dinner filled the house as we came home from school, church or just playing. But I also inherited the worrying until it breaks my heart.

I am that 'do whatever it takes to survive parent'....

Goodie or Jewel aka Ruby Jewel Turner, worked 40 hours a week plus was her work schedule. She battled all the elements of nature to do so as a soldier does. Never letting us go without our needs and provided some of our wants. Worked and worked and was already there when Busta and Nettie Lee was called home.

I inherited arrogance that can be considered good or bad....

Nate aka Nathan Turner from which I gained my hustle craft. Gotta do what it takes to survive these streets. Showing me that a man with a sensitive side is a man that's weak. But as he has gotten older his thoughts has changed. What he didn't give to me, I give to my children cause that's a father's job.

I am a man through hard work, household chores, long work hours and even my hustle. It's not just values I inherited but my faith in God which brings me through every day.

ANNOUNCEMENT

Calling all brothas

Uncle Sam wants you but your community needs you
Our children need their fathers everyday

Out having fun

Playing catch in the park
Protecting them when they get scared in the dark

Black warriors we need to unite and protect our fallen community
Stop making senseless violence a part of our community

Ridding our streets of drugs, prostitutes and gang banging
Embracing our lost brothas and sistas and begin rehabilitating
Our schools need us to step in and restructure our babies
Making schools safe for our children to be creative and learn daily

Instead of being safe on their way to school being their only concern
Religion is losing to the sin of these streets, when will we all learn

Collecting our families and take them back to church
Praying to be saved only during the perception behind the hearse

Calling all brothas
Yes this means you…..

Nolan Turner

BLACKMAN

I am a Blackman
From the tone of my voice
To the intellect that rolls off my lips
Sharing the blood of my Creator
Attempting to do His will
The sweat rolls of my brow earns my take home

I am a Blackman
That keeps the lights on in the house
And the food that grace my family's mouth
Ensuring proper clothing is on their backs
At night the chills don't visit their dreams
Or the body armor
That protects their well being

I am a Blackman
Not scared of hard work
Or to show my determination
Realizing that tough is sometimes being scared
And man enough to shed tears
Reliable enough to stay around
Dependable enough to stand my ground

I am a Blackman
Not willing to settle for anything
Learning how to get it all
I walk with power
Observing with purpose
Creating positive energy
Striving to make history

        I am a Blackman
        My skin tone identifies me
        My character defines me

LIFE TIME BID

1996 I found myself tied up in a situation. Now I'm serving a life time bid.
I'm real about mine. Yeah I did it, and take full responsibility for what I did

I pulled out my hot iron with no hesitation,
shooting 4 times over the years
I was sentenced and some thought it would destroy my mind
but it never did

Time that allowed me to reflect, I use to reflect and think.
Back against the wall, watching my surroundings
carefully I refused to blink

Responsible now for four lives. Yeah it's true I made it all happen
When their helpless voices cried out, I cried tears of excitement
and begun clappin'

No signs of remorse or regret for this lifetime bid
Because my end result was four beautiful kids...

STAGES

She….yes she was my girlfriend and I loved me some her
Shiny face, big teeth she belonged to me with that smile and dripping Jheri curl

Then her came along dark brown with a sassy attitude
But I wasn't a 'bad boy' so she chose another dude

This one yep, this one I thought was the one for me
But this one boyfriend came along and threatened to jump me in the streets

So came that one the world revolved around sun up and sun down but I was being a player and messed that up caused I was too busy fooling around

And finally came you; everything was going right in our world
never seen it coming when I found out that even you wasn't my girl….

But I know that
        She
        Her
        This one
        That one
        You

Prepared me for US!

AGING

Year after year I've watched people enter and leave my life
Returning to the Earth from which they came
Leaving emptiness inside that is everlasting
Even blowing into the breeze with "I'll be back"
Leaving nothing but memories behind

Year after year I mourn the loss that continuously plagues my heart
No more sunshine just rainy days piercing my skin
Causing endless scars that just never goes away
Scars that only the emotional eye can see

Year after year I've fought demons that roam through my soul
Feeling as if my pulse is the last it's as if the light becomes brighter
Only for the world to slowly fade away

Year after year I wonder if I'll be a memory
of someone or simply nothing at all

Nolan Turner

HONOR THY WOMAN

Honor thy woman like I honored my grandmother
Strong and supportive of all my decision,
Despite her better intuition
Sunday breakfast as church hymns play in our ears
Never showing her fears

Honor thy woman like I honored my mother
Refusing to fall to defeat
Even when called by the Lord she went strong even though being weak
Stern but yet sensitive to my needs
Reminding me to never lose focus on my dreams

Honor thy woman like I honored my Big Ma
Knew she loved me even when she frowned
By her I would sit when she signaled me to sit down
In her special chair I would watch her as she rest
When God called her home he took one of the best

Honor thy woman like I honor my sister
Crazy as a Betsy bug she's stays by my side
Never concerned she will die or ride
Through diversity she continues her hustles
Knowing with a phone call
I'm there on the double

Honor thy woman like I honor my music teacher
She embraced my bad ways and helped me find myself
By encouraging me to see my inner wealth
Instructing me on more than just singing
She taught me that I was better than a thug
I was a human being

Honor thy woman like I honor my friend of 22 years
Yes all the way back to Motorola pagers
She has always been there whether minor or major

HONOR THY WOMAN

We have seen each other shed a lot of tears
Rivers full from all the pain and happiness throughout the years

Honor thy woman like I honor the mother of my children
Through all the make ups and break ups our friendship withstand
When I'm down she extends her helping hand
Friend before all is who she is
Appreciating her drive and how she handles her business

Honor thy woman as I honor these women
Learning from them something different
Has contributed to making me a man and being better
Taught me to carry the weight on my back no matter the weather

Life lessons taught as well as learned
that respect for one another must be earned

Honor thy woman!

Nolan Turner

RAISED

I was raised by my mother, strong and as proud she was
taught me how to love my children with affection, kisses and hugs

I was raised by Busta, my Gramps, strict with a belt in his hand
learning that you fear no one but God and never any ma.

I was raised by Nettie Lee, Grandmama, by me she was
always called spiritual
taught me to keep God first in all my endeavors and
He'll catch me when I fall

I was raised by my father although he hasn't seen a lot of me
Reminds me that in my children's lives I must remain consistent
that's the key

Ms. Ann was the neighbor in the first apartment window
who was never leaving that space
As a young boy I caught the bus home getting off to her smiling face

Darryl and Scootie raised me by protecting me early from the streets
'Listen to yo moms', 'stay yo lil ass in school' and 'don't give the
 streets yo last heartbeat'

The junkies at the corner store raised me as well
realizing that even drunk and high everybody has a story to tell

A no nonsense teacher, Alice Lloyd,
put her ingredients in the mixing pot
She showed me confidence, traveling, love and music
from her I learned alot

Mrs. Ambrose was my English teacher and she seasoned me
with proper grammar and my love for writing.
Bringing stories to life in reader's minds sounded so exciting

RAISED

College raised me, drinking, partying and half ass going to class
and racial intimidation

I could have been more successful; the above line is my excuse
 and my explanation

When Momma, Busta and Nettie Lee was called home
God was raising me to realize that I will never stand alone

He continues to bring all types of people in my life
therefore unto Him I give the praise

I will continue to learn from their lives and experiences
as I continue to be RAISED

Nolan Turner

WHERE I'M GOING

I don't look like what I've been through
Late night arguments, that keep you awake at night
Being placed in situations where 'NO' only means 'NO' to you

Feeling numb as the look of concern come across your face
Listen when they say they love you, just not enough
to be there doing labor
Single parenthood only adding to my stressful days

Tried love again but sex was the master plan
Baby number 2 still solo, wow, nothing changed
Pointless voids of pleasure became my playground

Tears at night cause this wasn't my dream as a child
As my knight rode in on a horse gleaming of purity
It seems as if my autobiography was being edited

Blinded by the heart, I paid more attention to your words
Just to realize we wasn't reading from the same book
But telling you that's not what the book said made you strike out

When I got hit I realized it was on purpose
only 3 kids later, plus 2; 5 and I fled
Slipping now and then allowing you in my Sealy Posturepedic
Waking up one day to realize a stranger was in my space

So when the door closed I left you on the other side
Now although you haven't heard it; I've never stopped praying
And God always listens I just never obeyed
but it was my belief in Him that kept me alive

That's why I don't look like what I've been through
but I like where I'm going

Lineage of A Country Boy

THINK

Laying in the bed as the light from the candles casts

Shadows around my room

The moons brightness pierces through the window blinds

Crickets I hear making mating calls in the background

A cool breeze blows in through the air vents, as the central air kicks in

The house settles, I hear faint noises that alerts my senses

Yet the silence of the night attracts my curiosity more than anything

The simple things we take for granted until it's gone away

As simple as being able to wake up to these simple pleasures

And just…..THINK

NO MO'

Ain't no mo' music bout romancing
It's all about freelancing
To end up with HIV
Death now you're planning

No mo' "I believe the children are our future"
It's no mo' school days
Mo' like future slaves
Unmarked graves
Parents suffering from lives they couldn't save

We lost that phrase "I do"
Running around confused
Family is less important than those new pair of shoes
Raising hands to abuse
So our people we just run around and use

Now you see it, now you don't is the ideal of family
It's now just a use to be
Daddy out hustling in the streets
Momma getting paid to stay off her feet
Babies raising babies before the milk dries from their teeth

As days go on it's another sad black song
Life is going all wrong
Heart beats getting shorter pain lingering on
Extinction of black people we're gone

MY DEEPEST FEAR

My deepest fear is waking up in the morning to the unknown
Things being so insane in the world leave one confused of what lies ahead

I try to do right in a world full of chaos
Today in the news another young brother slain in the hood

When I look in the mirror my blood is what I envisioned
My headstone being the stop sign where that bullet struck me

The cemetery that consumes my corpse is the streets
Sounds heard in the hood is celebration not mourning

Society quit caring when I was born and my race was revealed
No one wants to see you to succeed

So the road blocks are created in hopes that you will quit
The dream I had was destroyed when you continuously said I wouldn't make it
The unknown was consuming my being to the point I didn't think for myself

As much as the attempt was made the concrete secured my feet
I'm beginning to feel the water dancing over my body

But this ain't no party and the music sounds more like the organ of death
It hurts so bad I begin to pop pills in attempt to soothe the pain

But as I start to think about it, the fear is overwhelming
So I decided not to wake up at all

Nolan Turner

FUNERAL REUNION

I attempt to be excited when the calls came through
Imagining all the faces I would see old and new

Going South that was cool, haven't been there in a few
Gotta make arrangements, prepare myself getting on the road
in a day or two

Sun beaming in my eyes, better put on my sunglasses now
Thinkin' to myself while I drive, I know it's gonna be a large crowd

Can't wait to see my aunties, uncles, nephews and nieces
It's been a long time as my intensity increases

Reality begins to set in damn what a shock in my mind
Thinking of all the elders saying "when it's yo time, it's yo time"

Although it seems like yesterday us joking around
Pallbearer huh, now, I'm carrying you to the ground

Tears setting in mad and confused all together
Remembering the words "I'll stay in touch" or "yeah right you betta"

But those is words to pacify the brain
Voices speaking those words don't even remember yo name

Don't remember yo number nor do they recall your face
First one to speak when you are at the meeting place

A little upset maybe a tad bit bitter as well
Now it's time for the final prayer before the church rings the bells

New faces, same speeches, nothing has changed coming from their mouth
See them at the next funeral reunion from the South

TWO MINUTES

Proverbs 18:21 (KJ) states: Death and life are in the power of the tongue and they that love it shall eat its fruit.

If I make it to the Lords' gates before you….

>Don't say I was a good father but I loved my children

>Don't say I was religious but I loved God

>Don't say I was a good employee but I loved what I did

>Don't say I was financially stable but I did the best with my finances

>Don't say I had all that I wanted but had everything I needed

>Don't say I was a damn good son but I had a damn good mother

>Don't say I was a wonderful friend but I offered friendship

>Don't say I was a gracious giver but I shared what I had

>Don't say I was the best man I could be but I worked hard at being a better man

>Don't feel sorrow in the words you speak in those two minutes

>Don't spend a lot of time grieving in those final two minutes

>But rejoice in me being with God and making it to my finish!

Nolan Turner

HOME

There is never a true understanding

Why the Lord decision to call us home is determine

But His grace is mighty, as the path home was preplanned at conception

Taught to love, accept love and to nurture those that crosses our paths

Helps to prepare us for when the time comes

Smiles given that may not be understood

Embracing others even if you don't know the reason

Showing you in the mist of sorrow

Stand tall, hold your head up and try not to shed tears

For where I've been invited to is a place of no pain, no violence,

Nor sickness and my worries are all gone

As I smile and watch over you know that God has welcomed me home

HISTORICAL OAK

My roots and branches are attached to a historical oak tree
from a long long time ago

A tree that my ancestor was hung and died from
The same tree they hid behind when they were on the run

At the same time the historical oak provided shade
During the blistering sun rays
Drinking, quenching her thirst during rainy days

Providing homes for all creature that
Needed a place to go
Never wilting or dying away
Through rain, sleet or snow

Being proud and strong never
Showing defeat
Proudly given a branch or two
So that drums could create beats

This oak tree I love for the lives she has sprouted
Wisdom she offers, sometime is confusing
But her creations were never doubted

All the souls of the love ones who've past
She has absorbed in her heart
She tells stories so passionately
Making you feel like you're there

When the time come for this
knowledge to extend down to me
I'll start with passionate stories
of the historical oak tree

Nolan Turner

PERFECT DINNER

If I could plan the perfect dinner, it would be at a table set for twelve
At the head of the table would be my grandpa,
Leading our Father's prayer cause that's what HE did
Holding hands like we did when we were just kids

If I could plan the perfect dinner, it would be a table set for twelve
Looking down at the other end where my grandmother dwelled fussing
 At Grand Pops because I didn't wanna eat liver
The thought of it still makes my body quivers

If I could plan the perfect dinner, it would be a table set for twelve
Sitting next to my mom with the Afro hair and little petite hands cutting up the liver meat remembering being the last one at the table sometimes falling asleep

If I could plan the perfect dinner it would be a table set for twelve
With uncles and aunties telling their old school tales like "I use to change your diaper",
"You was so fat and round"
 "I use to have to say to you lil' boy get yo behind down"

If I could plan the perfect dinner it would be a table set for twelve
All my little cousins who I used to call bad as hell, just for the chance
To talk and bond would be nice sadly not the type of family to make that sacrifice

So I plan the perfect dinner at a table set for twelve
Surrounded by my kids, nieces and nephews at the end of the table
I dwell and the prayer I lead cause now that's what I do
 Cutting up the meat, but liver is not one of the foods

PERFECT DINNER

Kicking it with them about old school tales they didn't get to hear
while explaining it's important to make this sacrifice at least once a year

Most importantly, no matter where you dwell
remember there's no perfect dinner unless the table is set for twelve......

Open your eyes as the saga continues…….

I AM

I am a crazy singer who loves dogs.

I wonder what I will look like when I'm older

I hear the sounds of crickets in the night

I see the birds in the morning

I want a dog for my birthday

I am a crazy singer who likes dogs.

I pretend to fight supper villains at night

I feel that my bed is on a cloud

I touch my imaginary dog

I worry that someone is in trouble

I cry when a family member passes

    I am a crazy singer who loves dogs

    I understand that dogs can bite

    I say I believe in magic

    I dream that I am riding on cows

    I try to succeed in school

    I hope to get a scholarship to a musical college

    I am a crazy singer who likes dogs!

    Kristion Martin-Turner

THE DAYS

The days you age

The days you dance

The days you party

And it always seems fun

The days of laughter

The days of frosting

The days of an off day

And it always seems fun

The days of family

The days of dinner

The days of special occasions

And it all seems fun

The days, it is always a glorious day on your birthday and you always have a great time

MacKenzie Martin-Turner

Lineage of A Country Boy

FAMILY RECORD

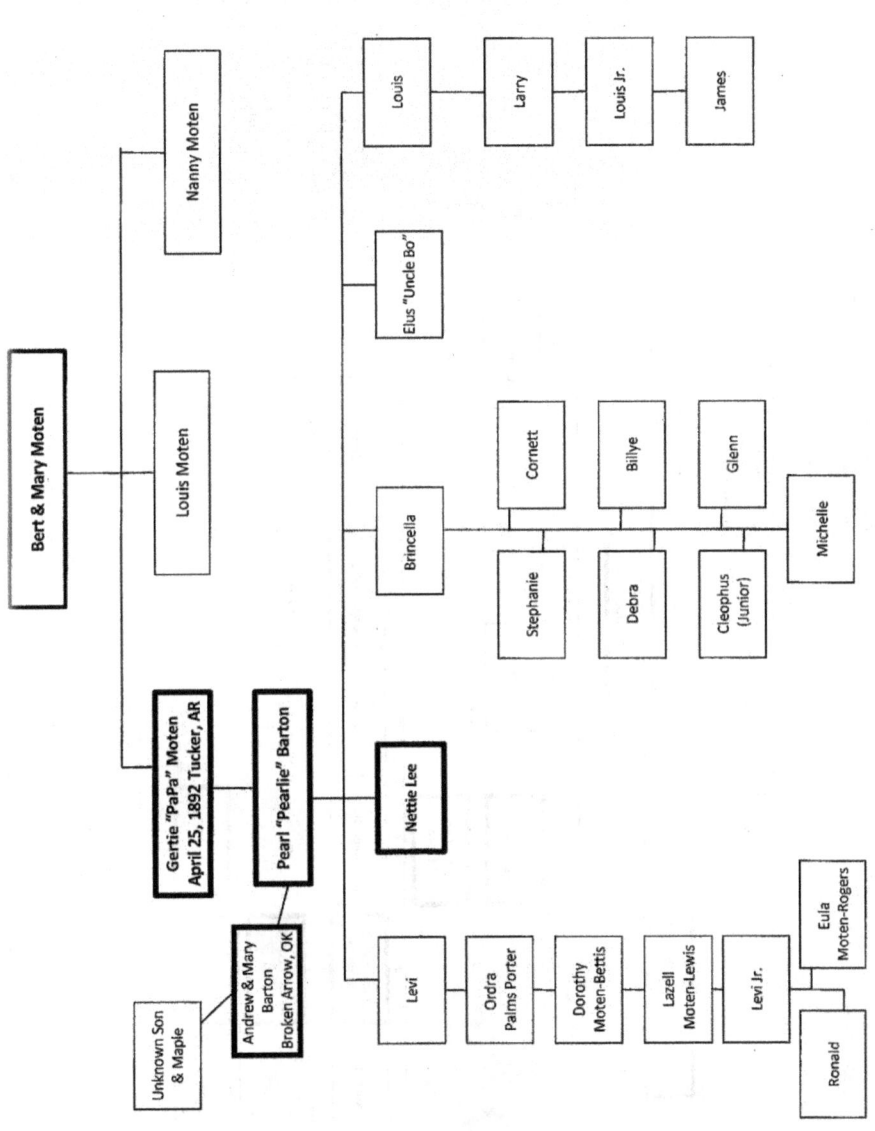

FAMILY RECORD

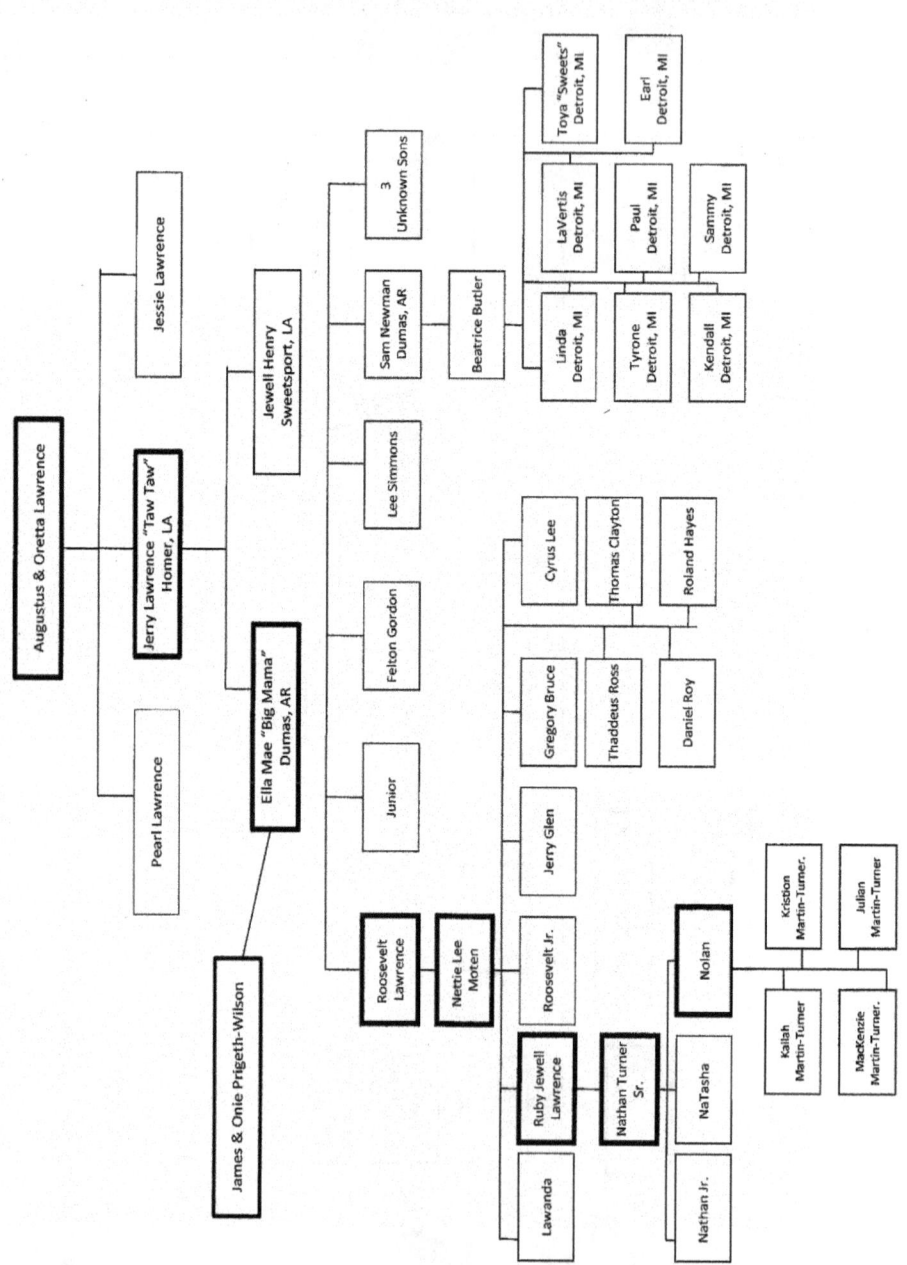

ABOUT THE AUTHOR

Nolan Turner also pens under the pseudo name of Blacklife. Nolan Turner is a native of Detroit, Michigan. He is also a proud product of the Detroit Public School System - Martin Luther King Jr. High School (Crusaders).

He developed his love for writing in the late nineties beginning with writing music that later evolved into a deeper love for poetry. His love for writing continues to increase. He is constantly reminding himself through his words that he can achieve anything by believing in himself and having faith in God.

He published his first book, *Blackbook*, in 2008 and his second book, *Pure Love*, in 2013. Nolan's goal with his poetry is to ensure there is a mixture of poems for everyone. Nolan wants young people to read his work and see that he was once a child with a dream, a vision that overcame obstacles, worked hard to make his dream come true. NEVER GIVE UP!

www.ingramcontent.com/pod-product-compliance
Lightning Source LLC
Chambersburg PA
CBHW050706160426
43194CB00010B/2021